God the Known and God the Unknown by Samuel Butler

Samuel Butler was born on 4th December 1835 at the village rectory in Langar, Nottinghamshire.

His relationship with his parents, especially his father, was largely antagonistic. His education began at home and included frequent beatings, as was all too common at the time.

Under his parents' influence, he was set to follow his father into the priesthood. He was schooled at Shrewsbury and then St John's College, Cambridge, where he obtained a first in Classics in 1858.

After Cambridge he went to live in a low-income parish in London 1858–59 as preparation for his ordination into the Anglican clergy; there he discovered that baptism made no apparent difference to the morals and behaviour of his new peers. He began to question his faith. Correspondence with his father about the issue failed to set his mind at peace, inciting instead his father's wrath.

As a result, the young Butler emigrated in September 1859 to New Zealand. He was determined to change his life.

He wrote of his arrival and life as a sheep farmer on Mesopotamia Station in 'A First Year in Canterbury Settlement' (1863). After a few years he sold his farm and made a handsome profit. But the chief achievement of these years were the drafts and source material for much of his masterpiece 'Erewhon'.

Butler returned to England in 1864, settling in rooms in Clifford's Inn, near Fleet Street, where he would live for the rest of his life.

In 1872, he published his Utopian novel 'Erewhon' which made him a well-known figure.

He wrote a number of other books, including a moderately successful sequel, 'Erewhon Revisited' before his masterpiece and semi-autobiographical novel 'The Way of All Flesh' appeared after his death. Butler thought its tone of satirical attack on Victorian morality too contentious to publish during his life time and thereby shied away from further potential problems.

Samuel Butler died aged 66 on 18th June 1902 at a nursing home in St John's Wood Road, London. He was cremated at Woking Crematorium, and accounts say his ashes were either dispersed or buried in an unmarked grave.

Index of Contents

Prefatory Note

"God the Known and God the Unknown" first appeared in the form of a series of articles which were published in "The Examiner" in May, June, and July, 1879. Samuel Butler subsequently revised the text of his work, presumably with the intention of republishing it, though he never carried the intention into effect. In the present edition I have followed his revised version almost without deviation. I have, however, retained a few passages which Butler proposed to omit, partly because they appear to me to render the course of his argument clearer, and partly because they contain characteristic thoughts and expressions of which none of his admirers would wish to be deprived. In the list of Butler's works "God the Known and God the Unknown" follows "Life and Habit," which appeared in 1877, and "Evolution, Old and New," which was published in May, 1879. It is scarcely necessary to point out that the three works are closely akin in subject and treatment, and that "God the Known and God the Unknown" will gain in interest by being considered in relation to its predecessors.

R. A. STREATFEILD

CHAPTER I

INTRODUCTION

Mankind has ever been ready to discuss matters in the inverse ratio of their importance, so that the more closely a question is felt to touch the hearts of all of us, the more incumbent it is considered upon prudent people to profess that it does not exist, to frown it down, to tell it to hold its tongue, to maintain that it has long been finally settled, so that there is now no question concerning it.

So far, indeed, has this been carried through all time past that the actions which are most important to us, such as our passage through the embryonic stages, the circulation of our blood, our respiration, etc. etc., have long been formulated beyond all power of reopening question concerning them—the mere fact or manner of their being done at all being ranked among the great discoveries of recent ages. Yet the analogy of past settlements would lead us to suppose that so much unanimity was not arrived at all at once, but rather that it must have been preceded by much smouldering discontent, which again was followed by open warfare; and that even after a settlement had been ostensibly arrived at, there was still much secret want of conviction on the part of many for several generations.

There are many who see nothing in this tendency of our nature but occasion for sarcasm; those, on the other hand, who hold that the world is by this time old enough to be the best judge concerning the management of its own affairs will scrutinise this management with some closeness before they venture to satirise it; nor will they do so for long without finding justification for its apparent recklessness; for we must all fear responsibility upon matters about which we feel we know but little; on the other hand we must all continually act, and for the most part promptly. We do so, therefore, with greater security when we can persuade both ourselves and others that a matter is already pigeon-holed than if we feel that we must use our own judgment for the collection, interpretation, and arrangement of the papers which deal with it. Moreover, our action is thus made to appear as if it received collective sanction; and by so appearing it receives it. Almost any settlement, again, is felt to be better than none, and the more nearly a matter comes home to everyone, the more important is it that it should be treated as a sleeping dog, and be let to lie, for if one person begins to open his mouth, fatal developments may arise in the Babel that will follow.

It is not difficult, indeed, to show that, instead of having reason to complain of the desire for the postponement of important questions, as though the world were composed mainly of knaves or fools, such fixity as animal and vegetable forms possess is due to this very instinct. For if there had been no reluctance, if there were no friction and vis inertae to be encountered even after a theoretical equilibrium had been upset, we should have had no fixed organs nor settled proclivities, but should have been daily and hourly undergoing Protean transformations, and have still been throwing out pseudopodia like the amoeba. True, we might have come to like this fashion of living as well as our more steady-going system if we had taken to it many millions of ages ago when we were yet young; but we have contracted other habits which have become so confirmed that we cannot break with them. We therefore now hate that which we should perhaps have loved if we had practised it. This, however, does not affect the argument, for our concern is with our likes and dislikes, not with the manner in which those likes and dislikes have come about. The discovery that organism is capable of modification at all has occasioned so much astonishment that it has taken the most enlightened part of the world more than a hundred years to leave off expressing its contempt for such a crude, shallow, and preposterous conception. Perhaps in another hundred years we shall learn to admire the good sense, endurance, and thorough Englishness of organism in having been so averse to change, even more than its versatility in having been willing to change so much.

Nevertheless, however conservative we may be, and however much alive to the folly and wickedness of tampering with settled convictions-no matter what they are-without sufficient cause, there is yet such a constant though gradual change in our surroundings as necessitates corresponding modification in our ideas, desires, and actions. We may think that we should like to find ourselves always in the same surroundings as our ancestors, so that we might be guided at every touch and turn by the experience of our race, and be saved from all self-communing or interpretation of oracular responses uttered by the facts around us. Yet the facts will change their utterances in spite of us; and we, too, change with age and ages in spite of ourselves, so as to see the facts around us as perhaps even more changed than they actually are. It has been said, "Tempora mutantur nos et mutamur in illis." The passage would have been no less true if it had stood, "Nos mutamur et tempora mutantur in nobis." Whether the organism or the surroundings began changing first is a matter of such small moment that the two may be left to fight it out between themselves; but, whichever view is taken, the fact will remain that whenever the relations between the organism and its surroundings have been changed, the organism must either succeed in putting the surroundings into harmony with itself, or itself into harmony with the surroundings; or must be made so uncomfortable as to be unable to remember itself as subjected to any such difficulties, and therefore to die through inability to recognise its own identity further.

Under these circumstances, organism must act in one or other of these two ways: it must either change slowly and continuously with the surroundings, paying cash for everything, meeting the smallest change with a corresponding modification so far as is found convenient; or it must put off change as long as possible, and then make larger and more sweeping changes.

Both these courses are the same in principle, the difference being only one of scale, and the one being a miniature of the other, as a ripple is an Atlantic wave in little; both have their advantages and disadvantages, so that most organisms will take the one course for one set of things and the other for another. They will deal promptly with things which they can get at easily, and which lie more upon the surface; those, however, which are more troublesome to reach, and lie deeper, will be handled upon more cataclysmic principles, being allowed longer periods of repose followed by short periods of greater activity.

Animals breathe and circulate their blood by a little action many times a minute; but they feed, some of them, only two or three times a day, and breed for the most part not more than once a year, their breeding season being much their busiest time. It is on the first principle that the modification of animal forms has proceeded mainly; but it may be questioned whether what is called a sport is not the organic expression of discontent which has been long felt, but which has not been attended to, nor been met step by step by as much small remedial modification as was found practicable: so that when a change does come it comes by way of revolution. Or, again (only that it comes to much the same thing), a sport may be compared to one of those happy thoughts which sometimes come to us unbidden after we have been thinking for a long time what to do, or how to arrange our ideas, and have yet been unable to arrive at any conclusion.

So with politics, the smaller the matter the prompter, as a general rule, the settlement; on the other hand, the more sweeping the change that is felt to be necessary, the longer it will be deferred.

The advantages of dealing with the larger questions by more cataclysmic methods are obvious. For, in the first place, all composite things must have a system, or arrangement of parts, so that some parts shall depend upon and be grouped round others, as in the articulation of a skeleton and the arrangement of muscles, nerves, tendons, etc., which are attached to it. To meddle with the skeleton is like taking up the street, or the flooring of one's house; it so upsets our arrangements that we put it off till whatever else is found wanted, or whatever else seems likely to be wanted for a long time hence, can be done at the same time. Another advantage is in the rest which is given to the attention during the long hollows, so to speak, of the waves between the periods of resettlement. Passion and prejudice have time to calm down, and when attention is next directed to the same question, it is a refreshed and invigorated attention-an attention, moreover, which may be given with the help of new lights derived from other quarters that were not luminous when the question was last considered. Thirdly, it is more easy and safer to make such alterations as experience has proved to be necessary than to forecast what is going to be wanted. Reformers are like paymasters, of whom there are only two bad kinds, those who pay too soon, and those who do not pay at all.

CHAPTER II

COMMON GROUND

I have now, perhaps, sufficiently proved my sympathy with the reluctance felt by many to tolerate discussion upon such a subject as the existence and nature of God. I trust that I may have made the reader feel that he need fear no sarcasm or levity in my treatment of the subject which I have chosen. I will, therefore, proceed to sketch out a plan of what I hope to establish, and this in no doubtful or unnatural sense, but by attaching the same meanings to words as those which we usually attach to them, and with the same certainty, precision, and clearness as anything else is established which is commonly called known.

As to what God is, beyond the fact that he is the Spirit and the Life which creates, governs, and upholds all living things, I can say nothing. I cannot pretend that I can show more than others have done in what Spirit and the Life consists, which governs living things and animates them. I cannot show the connection between consciousness and the will, and the organ, much less can I tear away the veil from the face of God, so as to show wherein will and consciousness consist. No philosopher, whether Christian or Rationalist, has attempted this without discomfiture; but I can, I hope, do two things: Firstly, I can demonstrate, perhaps more clearly than modern science is prepared to admit, that there does exist a single Being or Animator of all living things—a single Spirit, whom we cannot think of under any meaner name than God; and, secondly, I can show something more of the persona or bodily expression, mask, and mouthpiece of this vast Living Spirit than I know of as having been familiarly expressed elsewhere, or as being accessible to myself or others, though doubtless many works exist in which what I am going to say has been already said.

Aware that much of this is widely accepted under the name of Pantheism, I venture to think it differs from Pantheism with all the difference that exists between a coherent, intelligible conception and an incoherent unintelligible one. I shall therefore proceed to examine the doctrine called Pantheism, and to show how incomprehensible and valueless it is.

I will then indicate the Living and Personal God about whose existence and about many of whose attributes there is no room for question; I will show that man has been so far made in the likeness of this Person or God, that He possesses all its essential characteristics, and that it is this God who has called man and all other living forms, whether animals or plants, into existence, so that our bodies are the temples of His spirit; that it is this which sustains them in their life and growth, who is one with them, living, moving, and having His being in them; in whom, also, they live and move, they in Him and He in them; He being not a Trinity in Unity only, but an Infinity in Unity, and a Unity in an Infinity; eternal in time past, for so much time at least that our minds can come no nearer to eternity than this; eternal for the future as long as the universe shall exist; ever changing, yet the same yesterday, and to-day, and for ever. And I will show this with so little ambiguity that it shall be perceived not as a phantom or hallucination following upon a painful straining of the mind and a vain endeavour to give coherency to incoherent and inconsistent ideas, but with the same ease, comfort, and palpable flesh-and-blood clearness with which we see those near to us; whom, though we see them at the best as through a glass darkly, we still see face to face, even as we are ourselves seen.

I will also show in what way this Being exercises a moral government over the world, and rewards and punishes us according to His own laws.

Having done this I shall proceed to compare this conception of God with those that are currently accepted, and will endeavour to show that the ideas now current are in truth efforts to grasp the one on which I shall here insist. Finally, I shall persuade the reader that the differences between the so-called atheist and the so-called theist are differences rather about words than things, inasmuch as not even the most prosaic of modern scientists will be inclined to deny the existence of this God, while few theists will feel that this, the natural conception of God, is a less worthy one than that to which they have been accustomed.

CHAPTER III

PANTHEISM

The Rev. J. H. Blunt, in his "Dictionary of Sects, Heresies, etc.," defines Pantheists as "those who hold that God is everything, and everything is God."

If it is granted that the value of words lies in the definiteness and coherency of the ideas that present themselves to us when the words are heard or spoken-then such a sentence as "God is everything and everything is God" is worthless.

For we have so long associated the word "God" with the idea of a Living Person, who can see, hear, will, feel pleasure, displeasure, etc., that we cannot think of God, and also of something which we have not been accustomed to think of as a Living Person, at one and the same time, so as to connect the two ideas and fuse them into a coherent thought. While we are thinking of the one, our minds involuntarily exclude the other, and vice versa; so that it is as impossible for us to think of anything as God, or as forming part of God, which we cannot also think of as a Person, or as a part of a Person, as it is to produce a hybrid between two widely distinct animals. If I am not mistaken, the barrenness of inconsistent ideas, and the sterility of widely distant species or genera of plants and animals, are one in principle-sterility of hybrids being due to barrenness of ideas, and barrenness of ideas arising from inability to fuse unfamiliar thoughts into a coherent conception. I have insisted on this at some length in "Life and Habit," but can do so no further here. (Note: Butler returned to this subject in "Luck, or cunning?" which was originally published in 1887.)

In like manner we have so long associated the word "Person" with the idea of a substantial visible body, limited in extent, and animated by an invisible something which we call Spirit, that we can think of nothing as a person which does not also bring these ideas before us. Any attempt to make us imagine God as a Person who does not fulfil the conditions which our ideas attach to the word "person," is ipso facto atheistic, as rendering the word God without meaning, and therefore without reality, and therefore non-existent to us. Our ideas are like our organism, they will stand a vast amount of modification if it is effected slowly and without shock, but the life departs out of them, leaving the form of an idea without the power thereof, if they are jarred too rudely.

Any being, then, whom we can imagine as God, must have all the qualities, capabilities, and also all the limitations which are implied when the word "person" is used.

But, again, we cannot conceive of "everything" as a person. "Everything" must comprehend all that is to be found on earth, or outside of it, and we know of no such persons as this. When we say "persons" we intend living people with flesh and blood; sometimes we extend our conceptions to animals and plants, but we have not hitherto done so as generally as I hope we shall some day come to do. Below animals and plants we have never in any seriousness gone. All that we have been able to regard as personal has had what we can call a living body, even though that body is vegetable only; and this body has been tangible, and has been comprised within certain definite limits, or within limits which have at any rate struck the eye as definite. And every part within these limits has been animated by an unseen something which we call soul or spirit. A person must be a persona—that is to say, the living mask and mouthpiece of an energy saturating it, and speaking through it. It must be animate in all its parts.

But "everything" is not animate. Animals and plants alone produce in us those ideas which can make reasonable people call them "persons" with consistency of intention. We can conceive of each animal and of each plant as a person; we can conceive again of a compound person like the coral polypes, or like a tree which is composed of a congeries of subordinate persons, inasmuch as each bud is a separate and individual plant. We can go farther than this, and, as I shall hope to show, we ought to do so; that is to say, we shall find it easier and more agreeable with our other ideas to go farther than not; for we should see all animal and vegetable life as united by a subtle and till lately invisible ramification, so that all living things are one tree-like growth, forming a single person. But we cannot conceive of oceans, continents, and air as forming parts of a person at all; much less can we think of them as forming one person with the living forms that inhabit them.

To ask this of us is like asking us to see the bowl and the water in which three gold-fish are swimming as part of the gold-fish. We cannot do it any more than we can do something physically impossible. We can see the gold-fish as forming one family, and therefore as in a way united to the personality of the parents from which they sprang, and therefore as members one of another, and therefore as forming a single growth of gold-fish, as boughs and buds unite to form a tree; but we cannot by any effort of the imagination introduce the bowl and the water into the personality, for we have never been accustomed to think of such things as living and personal. Those, therefore, who tell us that "God is everything, and everything is God," require us to see "everything" as a person, which we cannot; or God as not a person, which again we cannot.

Continuing the article of Mr. Blunt from which I have already quoted, I read:—

"Linus, in a passage which has been preserved by Stobaeus, exactly expresses the notion afterwards adopted by Spinoza: 'One sole energy governs all things; all things are unity, and each portion is All; for of one integer all things were born; in the end of time all things shall again become unity; the unity of multiplicity.' Orpheus, his disciple, taught no other doctrine."

According to Pythagoras, "an adept in the Orphic philosophy," "the soul of the world is the Divine energy which interpenetrates every portion of the mass, and the soul of man is an efflux of that energy. The world, too, is an exact impress of the Eternal Idea, which is the mind of God." John Scotus Erigena taught that "all is God and God is all." William of Champeaux, again, two hundred years later, maintained that "all individuality is one in substance, and varies only in its non-essential accidents and transient properties." Amalric of Bena and David of Dinant followed the theory out "into a thoroughgoing Pantheism." Amalric held that "All is God and God is all. The Creator and the creature are one Being. Ideas are at once creative and created, subjective and objective. God is the end of all, and all return to Him. As every variety of humanity forms one manhood, so the world contains individual forms of one eternal essence." David of Dinant only varied upon this by "imagining a corporeal unity. Although body, soul, and eternal substance are three, these three are one and the same being."

Giordano Bruno maintained the world of sense to be "a vast animal having the Deity for its living soul." The inanimate part of the world is thus excluded from participation in the Deity, and a conception that our minds can embrace is offered us instead of one which they cannot entertain, except as in a dream, incoherently. But without such a view of evolution as was prevalent at the beginning of this century, it was impossible to see "the world of sense" intelligently, as forming "a vast animal." Unless, therefore, Giordano Bruno held the opinions of Buffon, Dr. Erasmus Darwin, and Lamarck, with more definiteness than I am yet aware of his having done, his contention must be considered as a splendid prophecy, but as little more than a prophecy. He continues, "Birth is expansion from the one centre of Life; life is its continuance, and death is the necessary return of the ray to the centre of light." This begins finely, but ends mystically. I have not, however, compared the English translation with the original, and must reserve a fuller examination of Giordano Bruno's teaching for another opportunity.

Spinoza disbelieved in the world rather than in God. He was an Acosmist, to use Jacobi's expression, rather than an Atheist. According to him, "the Deity and the Universe are but one substance, at the same time both spirit and matter, thought and extension, which are the only known attributes of the Deity."

My readers will, I think, agree with me that there is very little of the above which conveys ideas with the fluency and comfort which accompany good words. Words are like servants: it is not enough that we should have them-we must have the most able and willing that we can find, and at the smallest wages that will content them. Having got them we must make the best and not the worst of them. Surely, in the greater part of what has been quoted above, the words are barren letters only: they do not quicken within us and enable us to conceive a thought, such as we can in our turn impress upon dead matter, and mould that matter into another shape than its own, through the thought which has become alive within us. No offspring of ideas has followed upon them, or, if any at all, yet in such unwonted shape, and with such want of alacrity, that we loathe them as malformations and miscarriages of our minds. Granted that if we examine them closely we shall at length find them to embody a little germ of truth-that is to say, of coherency with our other ideas; but there is too little truth in proportion to the trouble necessary to get at it. We can get more truth, that is to say, more coherency-for truth and coherency are one-for less trouble in other ways.

But it may be urged that the beginnings of all tasks are difficult and unremunerative, and that later developments of Pantheism may be more intelligible than the earlier ones. Unfortunately, this is not the case. On continuing Mr. Blunt's article, I find the later Pantheists a hundredfold more perplexing than the earlier ones. With Kant, Schelling, Fichte, and Hegel, we feel that we are with men who have been decoyed into a hopeless quagmire; we understand nothing of their language-we doubt whether they understand themselves, and feel that we can do nothing with them but look at them and pass them by.

In my next chapter I propose to show the end which the early Pantheists were striving after, and the reason and naturalness of their error.

CHAPTER IV

PANTHEISM

The earlier Pantheists were misled by the endeavour to lay hold of two distinct ideas, the one of which was a reality that has since been grasped and is of inestimable value, the other a phantom which has misled all who have followed it. The reality is the unity of Life, the oneness of the guiding and animating spirit which quickens animals and plants, so that they are all the outcome and expression of a common mind, and are in truth one animal; the phantom is the endeavour to find the origin of things, to reach the fountain-head of all energy, and thus to lay the foundations on which a philosophy may be constructed which none can accuse of being baseless, or of arguing in a circle.

In following as through a thick wood after the phantom our forefathers from time to time caught glimpses of the reality, which seemed so wonderful as it eluded them, and flitted back again into the thickets, that they declared it must be the phantom they were in search of, which was thus evidenced as actually existing. Whereon, instead of mastering such of the facts they met with as could be captured easily-which facts would have betrayed the hiding-places of others, and these again of others, and so ad infinitum-they overlooked what was within their reach, and followed hotly through brier and brake after an imaginary greater prize.

Great thoughts are not to be caught in this way. They must present themselves for capture of their own free will, or be taken after a little coyness only. They are like wealth and power, which, if a man is not born to them, are the more likely to take him, the more he has restrained himself from an attempt to snatch them. They hanker after those only who have tamed their nearer thoughts. Nevertheless, it is impossible not to feel that the early Pantheists were true prophets and seers, though the things were unknown to them without which a complete view was unattainable. What does Linus mean, we ask ourselves, when he says:—"One sole energy governs all things"? How can one sole energy govern, we will say, the reader and the chair on which he sits? What is meant by an energy governing a chair? If by an effort we have made ourselves believe we understand something which can be better expressed by these words than by any others, no sooner do we turn our backs than the ideas so painfully collected fly apart again. No matter how often we go in search of them, and force them into juxtaposition, they prove to have none of that innate coherent power with which ideas combine that we can hold as true and profitable.

Yet if Linus had confined his statement to living things, and had said that one sole energy governed all plants and animals, he would have come near both to being intelligible and true. For if, as we now believe, all animals and plants are descended from a single cell, they must be considered as cousins to one another, and as forming a single tree-like animal, every individual plant or animal of which is as truly one and the same person with the primordial cell as the oak a thousand years old is one and the same plant with the acorn out of which it has grown. This is easily understood, but will, I trust, be made to appear simpler presently.

When Linus says, "All things are unity, and each portion is All; for of one integer all things were born," it is impossible for plain people-who do not wish to use words unless they mean the same things by them as both they and others have been in the habit of meaning-to understand what is intended. How can each portion be all? How can one Londoner be all London? I know that this, too, can in a way be shown, but the resulting idea is too far to fetch, and when fetched does not fit in well enough with our other ideas to give it practical and commercial value. How, again, can all things be said to be born of one integer, unless the statement is confined to living things, which can alone be born at all, and unless a theory of evolution is intended, such as Linus would hardly have accepted?

Yet limit the "all things" to "all living things," grant the theory of evolution, and explain "each portion is All" to mean that all life is akin, and possesses the same essential fundamental characteristics, and it is surprising how nearly Linus approaches both to truth and intelligibility.

It may be said that the animate and the inanimate have the same fundamental substance, so that a chair might rot and be absorbed by grass, which grass might be eaten by a cow, which cow might be eaten by a man; and by similar processes the man might become a chair; but these facts are not presented to the mind by saying that "one energy governs all things"-a chair, we will say, and a man; we could only say that one energy governed a man and a chair, if the chair were a reasonable living person, who was actively and consciously engaged in helping the man to attain a certain end, unless, that is to say, we are to depart from all usual interpretation of words, in which case we invalidate the advantages of language and all the sanctions of morality.

"All things shall again become unity" is intelligible as meaning that all things probably have come from a single elementary substance, say hydrogen or what not, and that they will return to it; but the explanation of unity as being the "unity of multiplicity" puzzles; if there is any meaning it is too recondite to be of service to us.

What, again, is meant by saying that "the soul of the world is the Divine energy which interpenetrates every portion of the mass"? The soul of the world is an expression which, to myself, and, I should imagine, to most people, is without propriety. We cannot think of the world except as earth, air, and water, in this or that state, on and in which there grow plants and animals. What is meant by saying that earth has a soul, and lives? Does it move from place to place erratically? Does it feed? Does it reproduce itself? Does it make such noises, or commit such vagaries as shall make us say that it feels? Can it achieve its ends, and fail of achieving them through mistake? If it cannot, how has it a soul more than a dead man has a soul, out of whom we say that the soul has departed, and whose body we conceive of as returning to dead earth, inasmuch as it is now soulless? Is there any unnatural violence which can be done to our thoughts by which we can bring the ideas of a soul and of water, or of a stone into combination, and keep them there for long together? The ancients, indeed, said they believed their rivers to be gods, and carved likenesses of them under the forms of men; but even supposing this to have been their real mind, can it by any conceivable means become our own? Granted that a stone is kept from falling to dust by an energy which compels its particles to cohere, which energy can be taken out of it and converted into some other form of energy; granted (which may or may not be true) also, that the life of a living body is only the energy which keeps the particles which compose it in a certain disposition; and granted that the energy of the stone may be convertible into the energy of a living form, and that thus, after a long journey a tired idea may lag after the sound of such words as "the soul of the world." Granted all the above, nevertheless to speak of the world as having a soul is not sufficiently in harmony with our common notions, nor does it go sufficiently with the grain of our thoughts to render the expression a meaning one, or one that can be now used with any propriety or fitness, except by those who do not know their own meaninglessness. Vigorous minds will harbour vigorous thoughts only, or such as bid fair to become so; and vigorous thoughts are always simple, definite, and in harmony with everyday ideas.

We can imagine a soul as living in the lowest slime that moves, feeds, reproduces itself, remembers, and dies. The amoeba wants things, knows it wants them, alters itself so as to try and alter them, thus preparing for an intended modification of outside matter by a preliminary modification of itself. It thrives if the modification from within is followed by the desired modification in the external object; it knows that it is well, and breeds more freely in consequence. If it cannot get hold of outside matter, or cannot proselytise that matter and persuade it to see things through its own (the amoeba's) spectacles-if it cannot convert that matter, if the matter persists in disagreeing with it-its spirits droop, its soul is disquieted within it, it becomes listless like a withering flower-it languishes and dies. We cannot imagine a thing to live at all and yet be soulless except in sleep for a short time, and even so not quite soulless. The idea of a soul, or of that unknown something for which the word "soul" is our hieroglyphic, and the idea of living organism, unite so spontaneously, and stick together so inseparably, that no matter how often we sunder them they will elude our vigilance and come together, like true lovers, in spite of us. Let us not attempt to divorce ideas that have so long been wedded together.

I submit, then, that Pantheism, even as explained by those who had entered on the outskirts only of its great morass, nevertheless holds out so little hope of leading to any comfortable conclusion that it will be more reasonable to occupy our minds with other matter than to follow Pantheism further. The Pantheists speak of a person without meaning a person; they speak of a "him" and a "he" without having in their minds the idea of a living person with all its inevitable limitations. Pantheism is, therefore, as is said by Mr. Blunt in another article, "practically nothing else than Atheism; it has no belief in a personal deity overruling the affairs of the world, as Divine Providence, and is, therefore, Atheistic," and again, "Theism believes in a spirit superior to matter, and so does Pantheism; but the spirit of Theism is self-conscious, and therefore personal and of individual existence-a nature per se, and upholding all things by an active control; while Pantheism believes in spirit that is of a higher nature than brute matter, but is a mere unconscious principle of life, impersonal, irrational as the brute matter that it quickens."

If this verdict concerning Pantheism is true—and from all I can gather it is as nearly true as anything can be said to be which is predicated of an incoherent idea—the Pantheistic God is an attempt to lay hold of a truth which has nevertheless eluded its pursuers.

In my next chapter I will consider the commonly received, orthodox conception of God, and compare it with the Pantheistic. I will show that it, too, is Atheistic, inasmuch as, in spite of its professing to give us a conception of God, it raises no ideas in our minds of a person or Living Being—and a God who is not this is non-existent.

CHAPTER V

ORTHODOX THEISM

We have seen that Pantheism fails to satisfy, inasmuch as it requires us to mean something different by the word "God" from what we have been in the habit of meaning. I have already said-I fear, too often-that no conception of God can have any value or meaning for us which does not involve his existence as an independent Living Person of ineffable wisdom and power, vastness, and duration both in the past and for the future. If such a Being as this can be found existing and made evident, directly or indirectly, to human senses, there is a God. If otherwise, there is no God, or none, at any rate, so far as we can know, none with whom we need concern ourselves. No conscious personality, no God. An impersonal God is as much a contradiction in terms as an impersonal person.

Unfortunately, when we question orthodox theology closely, we find that it supposes God to be a person who has no material body such as could come within the range of any human sense, and make an impression upon it. He is supposed to be of a spiritual nature only, except in so far as one part of his triune personality is, according to the Athanasian Creed, "perfect man, of a reasonable soul and human flesh subsisting."

Here, then, we find ourselves in a dilemma. On the one hand, we are involved in the same difficulty as in the case of Pantheism, inasmuch as a person without flesh and blood, or something analogous, is not a person; we are required, therefore, to believe in a personal God, who has no true person; to believe, that is to say, in an impersonal person.

This, as we have seen already, is Atheism under another name, being, as it is, destructive of all idea of God whatever; for these words do not convey an idea of something which human intelligence can understand up to a certain point, and which it can watch going out of sight into regions beyond our view, but in the same direction-as we may infer other stars in space beyond the farthest that we know of; they convey utterly self-destructive ideas, which can have no real meaning, and can only be thought to have a meaning by ignorant and uncultivated people. Otherwise such foundation as human reason rests upon-that is to say, the current opinion of those whom the world appraises as reasonable and agreeable, or capable of being agreed with for any time-is sapped; the whole thing tumbles down, and we may have square circles and round triangles, which may be declared to be no longer absurdities and contradictions in terms, but mysteries that go beyond our reason, without being contrary to it. Few will maintain this, and those few may be neglected; an impersonal person must therefore be admitted to be nonsense, and an immaterial God to be Atheism in another shape.

On the other hand, if God is "of a reasonable soul and human flesh subsisting," and if he thus has the body without which he is-as far as we are concerned-non-existent, this body must yet be reasonably like other bodies, and must exist in some place and at some time. Furthermore, it must do sufficiently nearly what all other "human flesh" belonging to "perfect man" must do, or cease to be human flesh. Our ideas are like our organisms; they have some little elasticity and circumstance-suiting power, some little margin on which, as I have elsewhere said, side-notes may be written, and glosses on the original text; but this power is very limited. As offspring will only, as a general rule, vary very little from its immediate parents, and as it will fail either immediately or in the second generation if the parents differ too widely from one another, so we cannot get our idea of-we will say a horse-to conjure up to our minds the idea of any animal more unlike a horse than a pony is; nor can we get a well-defined idea of a combination between a horse and any animal more remote from it than an ass, zebra, or giraffe. We may, indeed, make a statue of a flying horse, but the idea is one which cannot be made plausible to any but ignorant people. So "human flesh" may vary a little from "human flesh" without undue violence being done to our reason and to the right use of language, but it cannot differ from it so much as not to eat, drink, nor waste and repair itself. "Human flesh," which is without these necessary adjuncts, is human flesh only to those who can believe in flying horses with feathered wings and bills like birds-that is to say, to vulgar and superstitious persons.

Lastly, not only must the "perfect man," who is the second person of the Godhead according to the orthodox faith, and who subsists of "human flesh" as well as of a "reasonable soul," not only must this person exist, but he must exist in some place either on this earth or outside it. If he exists on earth, he must be in Europe, Asia, Africa, America, or on some island, and if he were met with he must be capable of being seen and handled in the same way as all other things that can be called perfect man are seen; otherwise he is a perfect man who is not only not a perfect man, but who does not in any considerable degree resemble one. It is not, however, pretended by anyone that God, the "perfect man," is to be looked for in any place upon the surface of the globe.

If, on the other hand, the person of God exists in some sphere outside the earth, his human flesh again proves to be of an entirely different kind from all other human flesh, for we know that such flesh cannot exist except on earth; if in space unsupported, it must fall to the ground, or into some other planet, or into a sun, or go on revolving round the earth or some other heavenly body-or not be personal. None of those whose opinions will carry weight will assign a position either in some country on this earth, or yet again in space, to Jesus Christ, but this involves the rendering meaningless of all expressions which involve his personality.

The Christian conception, therefore, of the Deity proves when examined with any desire to understand our own meaning (and what lawlessness so great as the attempt to impose words upon our understandings which have no lawful settlement within them?) to be no less a contradiction in terms than the Pantheistic conception. It is Atheistic, as offering us a God which is not a God, inasmuch as we can conceive of no such being, nor of anything in the least like it. It is, like Pantheism, an illusion, which can be believed only by those who repeat a formula which they have learnt by heart in a foreign language of which they understand nothing, and yet aver that they believe it. There are doubtless many who will say that this is possible, but the majority of my readers will hold that no proposition can be believed or disbelieved until its nature is understood.

It may perhaps be said that there is another conception of God possible, and that we may see him as personal, without at the same time believing that he has any actual tangible existence. Thus we personify hope, truth, and justice, without intending to convey to anyone the impression that these qualities are women, with flesh and blood. Again, we do not think of Nature as an actual woman, though we call her one; why may we not conceive of God, then, as an expression whereby we personify, by a figure of speech only; the thing that is intended being no person, but our own highest ideal of power, wisdom, and duration.

There would be no reason to complain of this if this manner of using the word "God" were well understood. Many words have two meanings, or even three, without any mischievous confusion of thought following. There can not only be no objection to the use of the word God as a manner of expressing the highest ideal of which our minds can conceive, but on the contrary no better expression can be found, and it is a pity the word is not thus more generally used.

Few, however, would be content with any such limitation of God as that he should be an idea only, an expression for certain qualities of human thought and action. Whence, it may be fairly asked, did our deeply rooted belief in God as a Living Person originate? The idea of him as of an inconceivably vast, ancient, powerful, loving, and yet formidable Person is one which survives all changes of detail in men's opinion. I believe there are a few very savage tribes who are as absolutely without religious sense as the beasts of the field, but the vast majority for a long time past have been possessed with an idea that there is somewhere a Living God who is the Spirit and the Life of all that is, and who is a true Person with an individuality and self-consciousness of his own. It is only natural that we should be asked how such an idea has remained in the minds of so many—who differ upon almost every other part of their philosophy-for so long a time if it was without foundation, and a piece of dreamy mysticism only.

True, it has generally been declared that this God is an infinite God, and an infinite God is a God without any bounds or limitations; and a God without bounds or limitations is an impersonal God; and an impersonal God is Atheism. But may not this be the incoherency of prophecy which precedes the successful mastering of an idea? May we not think of this illusory expression as having arisen from inability to see the whereabouts of a certain vast but tangible Person as to whose existence men were nevertheless clear? If they felt that it existed, and yet could not say where, nor wherein it was to be laid hands on, they would be very likely to get out of the difficulty by saying that it existed as an infinite Spirit, partly from a desire to magnify what they felt must be so vast and powerful, and partly because they had as yet only a vague conception of what they were aiming at, and must, therefore, best express it vaguely.

We must not be surprised that when an idea is still inchoate its expression should be inconsistent and imperfect-ideas will almost always during the earlier history of a thought be put together experimentally so as to see whether or no they will cohere. Partly out of indolence, partly out of the desire of those who brought the ideas together to be declared right, and partly out of joy that the truth should be supposed found, incoherent ideas will be kept together longer than they should be; nevertheless they will in the end detach themselves and go, if others present themselves which fit into their place better. There is no consistency which has not once been inconsistent, nor coherency that has not been incoherent. The incoherency of our ideas concerning God is due to the fact that we have not yet truly found him, but it does not argue that he does not exist and cannot be found anywhere after more diligent search; on the contrary, the persistence of the main idea, in spite of the incoherency of its details, points strongly in the direction of believing that it rests upon a foundation in fact.

But it must be remembered there can be no God who is not personal and material: and if personal, then, though inconceivably vast in comparison with man, still limited in space and time, and capable of making mistakes concerning his own interests, though as a general rule right in his estimates concerning them. Where, then, is this Being? He must be on earth, or what folly can be greater than speaking of him as a person? What are persons on any other earth to us, or we to them? He must have existed and be going to exist through all time, and he must have a tangible body. Where, then, is the body of this God? And what is the mystery of his Incarnation?

It will be my business to show this in the following chapter.

CHAPTER VI

THE TREE OF LIFE

Atheism denies knowledge of a God of any kind. Pantheism and Theism alike profess to give us a God, but they alike fail to perform what they have promised. We can know nothing of the God they offer us, for not even do they themselves profess that any of our senses can be cognisant of him. They tell us that he is a personal God, but that he has no material person. This is disguised Atheism. What we want is a Personal God, the glory of whose Presence can be made in part evident to our senses, though what we can realise is less than nothing in comparison with what we must leave for ever unimagined.

And truly such a God is not far from every one of us; for if we survey the broader and deeper currents of men's thoughts during the last three thousand years, we may observe two great and steady sets as having carried away with them the more eligible races of mankind. The one is a tendency from Polytheism to Monotheism; the other from Polytypism to Monotypism of the earliest forms of life-all animal and vegetable forms having at length come to be regarded as differentiations of a single substance-to wit, protoplasm.

No man does well so to kick against the pricks as to set himself against tendencies of such depth, strength, and permanence as this. If he is to be in harmony with the dominant opinion of his own and of many past ages, he will see a single God-impregnate substance as having been the parent from which all living forms have sprung. One spirit, and one form capable of such modification as its directing spirit shall think fit; one soul and one body, one God and one Life.

For the time has come when the two unities so painfully arrived at must be joined together as body and soul, and be seen not as two, but one. There is no living organism untenanted by the Spirit of God, nor any Spirit of God perceivable by man apart from organism embodying and expressing it. God and the Life of the World are like a mountain, which will present different aspects as we look at it from different sides, but which, when we have gone all round it, proves to be one only. God is the animal and vegetable world, and the animal and vegetable world is God.

I have repeatedly said that we ought to see all animal and vegetable life as uniting to form a single personality. I should perhaps explain this more fully, for the idea of a compound person is one which at first is not very easy to grasp, inasmuch as we are not conscious of any but our more superficial aspects, and have therefore until lately failed to understand that we are ourselves compound persons. I may perhaps be allowed to quote from an earlier work.

"Each cell in the human body is now admitted by physiologists to be a person with an intelligent soul, differing from our own more complex soul in degree and not in kind, and, like ourselves, being born, living, and dying. It would appear, then, as though 'we,' 'our souls,' or 'selves,' or 'personalities,' or by whatever name we may prefer to be called, are but the consensus and full-flowing stream of countless sensations and impulses on the part of our tributary souls or 'selves,' who probably no more know that we exist, and that they exist as a part of us, than a microscopic insect knows the results of spectrum analysis, or than an agricultural labourer knows the working of the British Constitution; and of whom we know no more than we do of the habits and feelings of some class widely separated from our own." ("Life and Habit," p. 110.)

After which it became natural to ask the following question:—"Is it possible to avoid imagining that we may be ourselves atoms, undesignedly combining to form some vaster being, though we are utterly incapable of perceiving this being as a single individual, or of realising the scheme and scope of our own combination? And this, too, not a spiritual being, which, without matter or what we think matter of some sort, is as complete nonsense to us as though men bade us love and lean upon an intelligent vacuum, but a being with what is virtually flesh and blood and bones, with organs, senses, dimensions in some way analogous to our own, into some other part of which being at the time of our great change we must infallibly re-enter, starting clean anew, with bygones bygones, and no more ache for ever from age or antecedents.

"'An organic being,' writes Mr. Darwin, 'is a microcosm, a little universe, formed of a host of self-propagating organisms inconceivably minute and numerous as the stars in Heaven.' As these myriads of smaller organisms are parts and processes of us, so are we parts and processes of life at large."

A tree is composed of a multitude of subordinate trees, each bud being a distinct individual. So coral polypes form a tree-like growth of animal life, with branches from which spring individual polypes that are connected by a common tissue and supported by a common skeleton. We have no difficulty in seeing a unity in multitude, and a multitude in unity here, because we can observe the wood and the gelatinous tissue connecting together all the individuals which compose either the tree or the mass of polypes. Yet the skeleton, whether of tree or of polype, is inanimate; and the tissue, whether of bark or gelatine, is only the matted roots of the individual buds; so that the outward and striking connection between the individuals is more delusive than real. The true connection is one which cannot be seen, and consists in the animation of each bud by a like spirit-in the community of soul, in "the voice of the Lord which maketh men to be of one mind in an house"-"to dwell together in unity"-to take what are practically identical views of things, and express themselves in concert under all circumstances. Provided this-the true unifier of organism-can be shown to exist, the absence of gross outward and visible but inanimate common skeleton is no bar to oneness of personality.

Let us picture to our minds a tree of which all the woody fibre shall be invisible, the buds and leaves seeming to stand in mid-air unsupported and unconnected with one another, so that there is nothing but a certain tree-like collocation of foliage to suggest any common principle of growth uniting the leaves.

Three or four leaves of different ages stand living together at the place in the air where the end of each bough should be; of these the youngest are still tender and in the bud, while the older ones are turning yellow and on the point of falling. Between these leaves a sort of twig-like growth can be detected if they are looked at in certain lights, but it is hard to see, except perhaps when a bud is on the point of coming out. Then there does appear to be a connection which might be called branch-like.

The separate tufts are very different from one another, so that oak leaves, ash leaves, horse-chestnut leaves, etc., are each represented, but there is one species only at the end of each bough.

Though the trunk and all the inner boughs and leaves have disappeared, yet there hang here and there fossil leaves, also in mid-air; they appear to have been petrified, without method or selection, by what we call the caprices of nature; they hang in the path which the boughs and twigs would have taken, and they seem to indicate that if the tree could have been seen a million years earlier, before it had grown near its present size, the leaves standing at the end of each bough would have been found very different from what they are now. Let us suppose that all the leaves at the end of all the invisible boughs, no matter how different they now are from one another, were found in earliest budhood to be absolutely indistinguishable, and afterwards to develop towards each differentiation through stages which were indicated by the fossil leaves. Lastly, let us suppose that though the boughs which seem wanted to connect all the living forms of leaves with the fossil leaves, and with countless forms of which all trace has disappeared, and also with a single root-have become invisible, yet that there is irrefragable evidence to show that they once actually existed, and indeed are existing at this moment, in a condition as real though as invisible to the eye as air or electricity. Should we, I ask, under these circumstances hesitate to call our imaginary plant or tree by a single name, and to think of it as one person, merely upon the score that the woody fibre was invisible? Should we not esteem the common soul, memories and principles of growth which are preserved between all the buds, no matter how widely they differ in detail, as a more living bond of union than a framework of wood would be, which, though it were visible to the eye, would still be inanimate?

The mistletoe appears as closely connected with the tree on which it grows as any of the buds of the tree itself; it is fed upon the same sap as the other buds are, which sap-however much it may modify it at the last moment-it draws through the same fibres as do its foster-brothers-why then do we at once feel that the mistletoe is no part of the apple tree? Not from any want of manifest continuity, but from the spiritual difference-from the profoundly different views of life and things which are taken by the parasite and the tree on which it grows—the two are now different because they think differently—as long as they thought alike they were alike—that is to say they were protoplasm—they and we and all that lives meeting in this common substance.

We ought therefore to regard our supposed tufts of leaves as a tree, that is to say, as a compound existence, each one of whose component items is compounded of others which are also in their turn compounded. But the tree above described is no imaginary parallel to the condition of life upon the globe; it is perhaps as accurate a description of the Tree of Life as can be put into so small a compass. The most sure proof of a man's identity is the power to remember that such and such things happened, which none but he can know; the most sure proof of his remembering is the power to react his part in the original drama, whatever it may have been; if a man can repeat a performance with consummate truth, and can stand any amount of cross-questioning about it, he is the performer of the original performance, whatever it was. The memories which all living forms prove by their actions that they possess-the memories of their common identity with a single person in whom they meet-this is incontestable proof of their being animated by a common soul. It is certain, therefore, that all living forms, whether animal or vegetable, are in reality one animal; we and the mosses being part of the same vast person in no figurative sense, but with as much bona fide literal truth as when we say that a man's finger-nails and his eyes are parts of the same man.

It is in this Person that we may see the Body of God-and in the evolution of this Person, the mystery of His Incarnation.

[In "Unconscious Memory," Chapter V, Butler wrote: "In the articles above alluded to ("God the Known and God the Unknown") I separated the organic from the inorganic, but when I came to rewrite them I found that this could not be done, and that I must reconstruct what I had written." This reconstruction never having been effected, it may be well to quote further from "Unconscious Memory" (concluding chapter): "At parting, therefore, I would recommend the reader to see every atom in the universe as living and able to feel and remember, but in a humble way. He must have life eternal as well as matter eternal; and the life and the matter must be joined together inseparably as body and soul to one another. Thus he will see God everywhere, not as those who repeat phrases conventionally, but as people who would have their words taken according to their most natural and legitimate meaning; and he will feel that the main difference between him and many of those who oppose him lies in the fact that whereas both he and they use the same language, his opponents only half mean what they say, while he means it entirely... We shall endeavour to see the so-called inorganic as living, in respect of the qualities it has in common with the organic, rather than the organic as non-living in respect of the qualities it has in common with the inorganic."]

CHAPTER VII

THE LIKENESS OF GOD

In my last chapter I endeavoured to show that each living being, whether animal or plant, throughout the world is a component item of a single personality, in the same way as each individual citizen of a community is a member of one state, or as each cell of our own bodies is a separate person, or each bud of a tree a separate plant. We must therefore see the whole varied congeries of living things as a single very ancient Being, of inconceivable vastness, and animated by one Spirit.

We call the octogenarian one person with the embryo of a few days old from which he has developed. An oak or yew tree may be two thousand years old, but we call it one plant with the seed from which it has grown. Millions of individual buds have come and gone, to the yearly wasting and repairing of its substance; but the tree still lives and thrives, and the dead leaves have life therein. So the Tree of Life still lives and thrives as a single person, no matter how many new features it has acquired during its development, nor, again, how many of its individual leaves fall yellow to the ground daily. The spirit or soul of this person is the Spirit of God, and its body-for we know of no soul or spirit without a body, nor of any living body without a spirit or soul, and if there is a God at all there must be a body of God-is the many-membered outgrowth of protoplasm, the ensemble of animal and vegetable life.

To repeat. The Theologian of to-day tells us that there is a God, but is horrified at the idea of that God having a body. We say that we believe in God, but that our minds refuse to realise an intelligent Being who has no bodily person. "Where then," says the Theologian, "is the body of your God?" We have answered, "In the living forms upon the earth, which, though they look many, are, when we regard them by the light of their history and of true analogies, one person only." The spiritual connection between them is a more real bond of union than the visible discontinuity of material parts is ground for separating them in our thoughts.

Let the reader look at a case of moths in the shop-window of a naturalist, and note the unspeakable delicacy, beauty, and yet serviceableness of their wings; or let him look at a case of humming-birds, and remember how infinitely small a part of Nature is the whole group of the animals he may be considering, and how infinitely small a part of that group is the case that he is looking at. Let him bear in mind that he is looking on the dead husks only of what was inconceivably more marvellous when the moths or humming-birds were alive. Let him think of the vastness of the earth, and of the activity by day and night through countless ages of such countless forms of animal and vegetable life as that no human mind can form the faintest approach to anything that can be called a conception of their multitude, and let him remember that all these forms have touched and touched and touched other living beings till they meet back on a common substance in which they are rooted, and from which they all branch forth so as to be one animal. Will he not in this real and tangible existence find a God who is as much more worthy of admiration than the God of the ordinary Theologian-as He is also more easy of comprehension?

For the Theologian dreams of a God sitting above the clouds among the cherubim, who blow their loud uplifted angel trumpets before Him, and humour Him as though He were some despot in an Oriental tale; but we enthrone Him upon the wings of birds, on the petals of flowers, on the faces of our friends, and upon whatever we most delight in of all that lives upon the earth. We then can not only love Him, but we can do that without which love has neither power nor sweetness, but is a phantom only, an impersonal person, a vain stretching forth of arms towards something that can never fill them-we can express our love and have it expressed to us in return. And this not in the uprearing of stone temples-for the Lord dwelleth in temples made with other organs than hands-nor yet in the cleansing of our hearts, but in the caress bestowed upon horse and dog, and kisses upon the lips of those we love.

Wide, however, as is the difference between the orthodox Theologian and ourselves, it is not more remarkable than the number of the points on which we can agree with him, and on which, moreover, we can make his meaning clearer to himself than it can have ever hitherto been. He, for example, says that man has been made in the image of God, but he cannot mean what he says, unless his God has a material body; we, on the other hand, do not indeed believe that the body of God-the incorporation of all life-is like the body of a man, more than we believe each one of our own cells or subordinate personalities to be like a man in miniature; but we nevertheless hold that each of our tributary selves is so far made after the likeness of the body corporate that it possesses all our main and essential characteristics-that is to say, that it can waste and repair itself; can feel, move, and remember. To this extent, also, we-who stand in mean proportional between our tributary personalities and God-are made in the likeness of God; for we, and God, and our subordinate cells alike possess the essential characteristics of life which have been above recited. It is more true, therefore, for us to say that we are made in the likeness of God than for the orthodox Theologian to do so.

Nor, again, do we find difficulty in adopting such an expression as that "God has taken our nature upon Him." We hold this as firmly, and much more so, than Christians can do, but we say that this is no new thing for Him to do, for that He has taken flesh and dwelt among us from the day that He first assumed our shape, some millions of years ago, until now. God cannot become man more especially than He can become other living forms, any more than we can be our eyes more especially than any other of our organs. We may develop larger eyes, so that our eyes may come to occupy a still more important place in our economy than they do at present; and in a similar way the human race may become a more predominant part of God than it now is-but we cannot admit that one living form is more like God than another; we must hold all equally like Him, inasmuch as they "keep ever," as Buffon says, "the same fundamental unity, in spite of differences of detail-nutrition, development, reproduction" (and, I would add, "memory") "being the common traits of all organic bodies." The utmost we can admit is, that some embodiments of the Spirit of Life may be more important than others to the welfare of Life as a whole, in the same way as some of our organs are more important than others to ourselves.

But the above resemblances between the language which we can adopt intelligently and that which Theologians use vaguely, seem to reduce the differences of opinion between the two contending parties to disputes about detail. For even those who believe their ideas to be the most definite, and who picture to themselves a God as anthropomorphic as He was represented by Raffaelle, are yet not prepared to stand by their ideas if they are hard pressed in the same way as we are by ours. Those who say that God became man and took flesh upon Him, and that He is now perfect God and perfect man of a reasonable soul and human flesh subsisting, will yet not mean that Christ has a heart, blood, a stomach, etc., like man's, which, if he has not, it is idle to speak of him as "perfect man." I am persuaded that they do not mean this, nor wish to mean it; but that they have been led into saying it by a series of steps which it is very easy to understand and sympathise with, if they are considered with any diligence.

For our forefathers, though they might and did feel the existence of a Personal God in the world, yet could not demonstrate this existence, and made mistakes in their endeavour to persuade themselves that they understood thoroughly a truth which they had as yet perceived only from a long distance. Hence all the dogmatism and theology of many centuries. It was impossible for them to form a clear or definite conception concerning God until they had studied His works more deeply, so as to grasp the idea of many animals of different kinds and with no apparent connection between them, being yet truly parts of one and the same animal which comprised them in the same way as a tree comprises all its buds. They might speak of this by a figure of speech, but they could not see it as a fact. Before this could be intended literally, Evolution must be grasped, and not Evolution as taught in what is now commonly called Darwinism, but the old teleological Darwinism of eighty years ago. Nor is this again sufficient, for it must be supplemented by a perception of the oneness of personality between parents and offspring, the persistence of memory through all generations, the latency of this memory until rekindled by the recurrence of the associated ideas, and the unconsciousness with which repeated acts come to be performed. These are modern ideas which might be caught sight of now and again by prophets in time past, but which are even now mastered and held firmly only by the few.

When once, however, these ideas have been accepted, the chief difference between the orthodox God and the God who can be seen of all men is, that the first is supposed to have existed from all time, while the second has only lived for more millions of years than our minds can reckon intelligently; the first is omnipresent in all space, while the second is only present in the living forms upon this earth-that is to say, is only more widely present than our minds can intelligently embrace. The first is omnipotent and all-wise; the second is only quasi-omnipotent and quasi all-wise. It is true, then, that we deprive God of that infinity which orthodox Theologians have ascribed to Him, but the bounds we leave Him are of such incalculable extent that nothing can be imagined more glorious or vaster; and in return for the limitations we have assigned to Him, we render it possible for men to believe in Him, and love Him, not with their lips only, but with their hearts and lives.

Which, I may now venture to ask my readers, is the true God-the God of the Theologian, or He whom we may see around us, and in whose presence we stand each hour and moment of our lives?

CHAPTER VIII

THE LIFE EVERLASTING

Let us now consider the life which we can look forward to with certainty after death, and the moral government of the world here on earth.

If we could hear the leaves complaining to one another that they must die, and commiserating the hardness of their lot in having ever been induced to bud forth, we should, I imagine, despise them for their peevishness more than we should pity them. We should tell them that though we could not see reason for thinking that they would ever hang again upon the same-or any at all similar-bough as the same individual leaves, after they had once faded and fallen off, yet that as they had been changing personalities without feeling it during the whole of their leafhood, so they would on death continue to do this selfsame thing by entering into new phases of life. True, death will deprive them of conscious memory concerning their now current life; but, though they die as leaves, they live in the tree whom they have helped to vivify, and whose growth and continued well-being is due solely to this life and death of its component personalities.

We consider the cells which are born and die within us yearly to have been sufficiently honoured in having contributed their quotum to our life; why should we have such difficulty in seeing that a healthy enjoyment and employment of our life will give us a sufficient reward in that growth of God wherein we may live more truly and effectually after death than we have lived when we were conscious of existence? Is Handel dead when he influences and sets in motion more human beings in three months now than during the whole, probably, of the years in which he thought that he was alive? What is being alive if the power to draw men for many miles in order that they may put themselves en rapport with him is not being so? True, Handel no longer knows the power which he has over us, but this is a small matter; he no longer animates six feet of flesh and blood, but he lives in us as the dead leaf lives in the tree. He is with God, and God knows him though he knows himself no more.

This should suffice, and I observe in practice does suffice, for all reasonable persons. It may be said that one day the tree itself must die, and the leaves no longer live therein; and so, also, that the very God or Life of the World will one day perish, as all that is born must surely in the end die. But they who fret upon such grounds as this must be in so much want of a grievance that it were a cruelty to rob them of one: if a man who is fond of music tortures himself on the ground that one day all possible combinations and permutations of sounds will have been exhausted so that there can be no more new tunes, the only thing we can do with him is to pity him and leave him; nor is there any better course than this to take with those idle people who worry themselves and others on the score that they will one day be unable to remember the small balance of their lives that they have not already forgotten as unimportant to them-that they will one day die to the balance of what they have not already died to. I never knew a well-bred or amiable person who complained seriously of the fact that he would have to die. Granted we must all sometimes find ourselves feeling sorry that we cannot remain for ever at our present age, and that we may die so much sooner than we like; but these regrets are passing with well-disposed people, and are a sine qua non for the existence of life at all. For if people could live for ever so as to suffer from no such regret, there would be no growth nor development in life; if, on the other hand, there were no unwillingness to die, people would commit suicide upon the smallest contradiction, and the race would end in a twelvemonth.

We then offer immortality, but we do not offer resurrection from the dead; we say that those who die live in the Lord whether they be just or unjust, and that the present growth of God is the outcome of all past lives; but we believe that as they live in God-in the effect they have produced upon the universal life-when once their individual life is ended, so it is God who knows of their life thenceforward and not themselves; and we urge that this immortality, this entrance into the joy of the Lord, this being ever with God, is true, and can be apprehended by all men, and that the perception of it should and will tend to make them lead happier, healthier lives; whereas the commonly received opinion is true with a stage truth only, and has little permanent effect upon those who are best worth considering. Nevertheless the expressions in common use among the orthodox fit in so perfectly with facts, which we must all acknowledge, that it is impossible not to regard the expressions as founded upon a prophetic perception of the facts.

Two things stand out with sufficient clearness. The first is the rarity of suicide even among those who rail at life most bitterly. The other is the little eagerness with which those who cry out most loudly for a resurrection desire to begin their new life. When comforting a husband upon the loss of his wife we do not tell him we hope he will soon join her; but we should certainly do this if we could even pretend we thought the husband would like it. I can never remember having felt or witnessed any pain, bodily or mental, which would have made me or anyone else receive a suggestion that we had better commit suicide without indignantly asking how our adviser would like to commit suicide himself. Yet there are so many and such easy ways of dying that indignation at being advised to commit suicide arises more from enjoyment of life than from fear of the mere physical pain of dying. Granted that there is much deplorable pain in the world from ill-health, loss of money, loss of reputation, misconduct of those nearest to us, or what not, and granted that in some cases these causes do drive men to actual self-destruction, yet suffering such as this happens to a comparatively small number, and occupies comparatively a small space in the lives of those to whom it does happen.

What, however, have we to say to those cases in which suffering and injustice are inflicted upon defenceless people for years and years, so that the iron enters into their souls, and they have no avenger. Can we give any comfort to such sufferers? and, if not, is our religion any better than a mockery-a filling the rich with good things and sending the hungry empty away? Can we tell them, when they are oppressed with burdens, yet that their cry will come up to God and be heard? The question suggests its own answer, for assuredly our God knows our innermost secrets: there is not a word in our hearts but He knoweth it altogether; He knoweth our down-sitting and our uprising, He is about our path and about our bed, and spieth out all our ways; He has fashioned us behind and before, and "we cannot attain such knowledge," for, like all knowledge when it has become perfect, "it is too excellent for us."

"Whither then," says David, "shall I go from thy Spirit, or whither shall I go, then, from thy presence? If I climb up into heaven thou art there; if I go down into hell thou art there also. If I take the wings of the morning and remain in the uttermost parts of the sea; even there also shall thy hand lead me, and thy right hand shall hold me. If I say peradventure the darkness shall cover me, then shall my night be turned into day: the darkness and light to thee are both alike. For my reins are thine; thou hast covered me in my mother's womb. My bones are not hid from thee: though I be made secretly and fashioned beneath in the earth, thine eyes did see my substance yet being unperfect; and in thy book were all my members written, which day by day were fashioned when as yet there was none of them. Do I not hate them, O Lord, that hate thee? and am I not grieved with them that rise up against thee? Yea, I hate them right sore, as though they were mine enemies." (Psalm CXXXIX.) There is not a word of this which we cannot endorse with more significance, as well as with greater heartiness than those can who look upon God as He is commonly represented to them; whatever comfort, therefore, those in distress have been in the habit of receiving from these and kindred passages, we intensify rather than not. We cannot, alas! make pain cease to be pain, nor injustice easy to bear; but we can show that no pain is bootless, and that there is a tendency in all injustice to right itself; suffering is not inflicted wilfully, as it were by a magician who could have averted it; nor is it vain in its results, but unless we are cut off from God by having dwelt in some place where none of our kind can know of what has happened to us, it will move God's heart to redress our grievance, and will tend to the happiness of those who come after us, even if not to our own.

The moral government of God over the world is exercised through us, who are his ministers and persons, and a government of this description is the only one which can be observed as practically influencing men's conduct. God helps those who help themselves, because in helping themselves they are helping Him. Again, Vox Populi vox Dei. The current feeling of our peers is what we instinctively turn to when we would know whether such and such a course of conduct is right or wrong; and so Paul clenches his list of things that the Philippians were to hold fast with the words, "whatsoever things are of good fame"-that is to say, he falls back upon an appeal to the educated conscience of his age. Certainly the wicked do sometimes appear to escape punishment, but it must be remembered there are punishments from within which do not meet the eye. If these fall on a man, he is sufficiently punished; if they do not fall on him, it is probable we have been over hasty in assuming that he is wicked.

CHAPTER IX

GOD THE UNKNOWN

The reader will already have felt that the panzoistic conception of God-the conception, that is to say, of God as comprising all living units in His own single person-does not help us to understand the origin of matter, nor yet that of the primordial cell which has grown and unfolded itself into the present life of the world. How was the world rendered fit for the habitation of the first germ of Life? How came it to have air and water, without which nothing that we know of as living can exist? Was the world fashioned and furnished with aqueous and atmospheric adjuncts with a view to the requirements of the infant monad, and to his due development? If so, we have evidence of design, and if so of a designer, and if so there must be Some far vaster Person who looms out behind our God, and who stands in the same relation to him as he to us. And behind this vaster and more unknown God there may be yet another, and another, and another.

It is certain that Life did not make the world with a view to its own future requirements. For the world was at one time red hot, and there can have been no living being upon it. Nor is it conceivable that matter in which there was no life-inasmuch as it was infinitely hotter than the hottest infusion which any living germ can support-could gradually come to be alive without impregnation from a living parent. All living things that we know of have come from other living things with bodies and souls, whose existence can be satisfactorily established in spite of their being often too small for our detection. Since, then, the world was once without life, and since no analogy points in the direction of thinking that life can spring up spontaneously, we are driven to suppose that it was introduced into this world from some other source extraneous to it altogether, and if so we find ourselves irresistibly drawn to the inquiry whether the source of the life that is in the world-the impregnator of this earth-may not also have prepared the earth for the reception of his offspring, as a hen makes an egg-shell or a peach a stone for the protection of the germ within it? Not only are we drawn to the inquiry, but we are drawn also to the answer that the earth was so prepared designedly by a Person with body and soul who knew beforehand the kind of thing he required, and who took the necessary steps to bring it about.

If this is so we are members indeed of the God of this world, but we are not his children; we are children of the Unknown and Vaster God who called him into existence; and this in a far more literal sense than we have been in the habit of realising to ourselves. For it may be doubted whether the monads are not as truly seminal in character as the procreative matter from which all animals spring.

It must be remembered that if there is any truth in the view put forward in "Life and Habit," and in "Evolution Old and New" (and I have met with no serious attempt to upset the line of argument taken in either of these books), then no complex animal or plant can reach its full development without having already gone through the stages of that development on an infinite number of past occasions. An egg makes itself into a hen because it knows the way to do so, having already made itself into a hen millions and millions of times over; the ease and unconsciousness with which it grows being in themselves sufficient demonstration of this fact. At each stage in its growth the chicken is reminded, by a return of the associated ideas, of the next step that it should take, and it accordingly takes it.

But if this is so, and if also the congeries of all the living forms in the world must be regarded as a single person, throughout their long growth from the primordial cell onwards to the present day, then, by parity of reasoning, the person thus compounded-that is to say, Life or God-should have already passed through a growth analogous to that which we find he has taken upon this earth on an infinite number of past occasions; and the development of each class of life, with its culmination in the vertebrate animals and in man, should be due to recollection by God of his having passed through the same stages, or nearly so, in worlds and universes, which we know of from personal recollection, as evidenced in the growth and structure of our bodies, but concerning which we have no other knowledge whatsoever.

So small a space remains to me that I cannot pursue further the reflections which suggest themselves. A few concluding considerations are here alone possible.

We know of three great concentric phases of life, and we are not without reason to suspect a fourth. If there are so many there are very likely more, but we do not know whether there are or not. The innermost sphere of life we know of is that of our own cells. These people live in a world of their own, knowing nothing of us, nor being known by ourselves until very recently. Yet they can be seen under a microscope; they can be taken out of us, and may then be watched going here and there in perturbation of mind, endeavouring to find something in their new environment that will suit them, and then dying on finding how hopelessly different it is from any to which they have been accustomed. They live in us, and make us up into the single person which we conceive ourselves to form; we are to them a world comprising an organic and an inorganic kingdom, of which they consider themselves to be the organic, and whatever is not very like themselves to be the inorganic. Whether they are composed of subordinate personalities or not we do not know, but we have no reason to think that they are, and if we touch ground, so to speak, with life in the units of which our own bodies are composed, it is likely that there is a limit also in an upward direction, though we have nothing whatever to guide us as to where it is, nor any certainty that there is a limit at all.

We are ourselves the second concentric sphere of life, we being the constituent cells which unite to form the body of God. Of the third sphere we know a single member only-the God of this world; but we see also the stars in heaven, and know their multitude. Analogy points irresistibly in the direction of thinking that these other worlds are like our own, begodded and full of life; it also bids us believe that the God of their world is begotten of one more or less like himself, and that his growth has followed the same course as that of all other growths we know of.

If so, he is one of the constituent units of an unknown and vaster personality who is composed of Gods, as our God is composed of all the living forms on earth, and as all those living forms are composed of cells. This is the Unknown God. Beyond this second God we cannot at present go, nor should we wish to do so, if we are wise. It is no reproach to a system that it does not profess to give an account of the origin of things; the reproach rather should lie against a system which professed to explain it, for we may be well assured that such a profession would, for the present at any rate, be an empty boast. It is enough if a system is true as far as it goes; if it throws new light on old problems, and opens up vistas which reveal a hope of further addition to our knowledge, and this I believe may be fairly claimed for the theory of life put forward in "Life and Habit" and "Evolution, Old and New," and for the corollary insisted upon in these pages; a corollary which follows logically and irresistibly if the position I have taken in the above-named books is admitted.

Let us imagine that one of the cells of which we are composed could attain to a glimmering perception of the manner in which he unites with other cells, of whom he knows very little, so as to form a greater compound person of whom he has hitherto known nothing at all. Would he not do well to content himself with the mastering of this conception, at any rate for a considerable time? Would it be any just ground of complaint against him on the part of his brother cells, that he had failed to explain to them who made the man (or, as he would call it, the omnipotent deity) whose existence and relations to himself he had just caught sight of?

But if he were to argue further on the same lines as those on which he had travelled hitherto, and were to arrive at the conclusion that there might be other men in the world. besides the one whom he had just learnt to apprehend, it would be still no refutation or just ground of complaint against him that he had failed to show the manner in which his supposed human race had come into existence.

Here our cell would probably stop. He could hardly be expected to arrive at the existence of animals and plants differing from the human race, and uniting with that race to form a single Person or God, in the same way as he has himself united with other cells to form man. The existence, and much more the roundness of the earth itself, would be unknown to him, except by way of inference and deduction. The only universe which he could at all understand would be the body of the man of whom he was a component part.

How would not such a cell be astounded if all that we know ourselves could be suddenly revealed to him, so that not only should the vastness of this earth burst upon his dazzled view, but that of the sun and of his planets also, and not only these, but the countless other suns which we may see by night around us. Yet it is probable that an actual being is hidden from us, which no less transcends the wildest dream of our theologians than the existence of the heavenly bodies transcends the perception of our own constituent cells.

Samuel Butler – A Short Biography

Samuel Butler was born on 4th December 1835 at the village rectory in Langar, Nottinghamshire, to the Rev. Thomas Butler, himself the son of Dr. Samuel Butler, then headmaster of Shrewsbury School and later Bishop of Lichfield.

The young Butler's immediate family created an oppressive home environment that was largely antagonistic (he later chronicled this in 'The Way of All Flesh'). It was said that Thomas Butler, to make up for having been a servile son, became a bullying and overbearing father. The relationship with his mother was better, but not by much.

His education began at home and included frequent beatings, as was all too common at the time. Samuel wrote later that his parents were "brutal and stupid by nature." He later wrote that his father "never liked me, nor I him; from my earliest recollections I can call to mind no time when I did not fear him and dislike him .... I have never passed a day without thinking of him many times over as the man who was sure to be against me."

Under his parents' parochial influence, he was set to follow his father into the priesthood. He was sent to Shrewsbury at the age of twelve, where he did not enjoy the hard life and its routines.

From there, in 1854, he went to St John's College, Cambridge, where he obtained a first in Classics in 1858. The graduate society of St John's was later named the Samuel Butler Room in his honour.

After Cambridge he went to live in an impoverished parish in London 1858–59 as preparation for his ordination into the Anglican clergy; there he uneasily discovered that baptism made no apparent difference to the morals and behaviour of his new peers. He began to question his faith. This experience would later serve as inspiration for his work 'The Fair Haven'. His correspondence with his father about the issue failed to set his mind at rest, inciting instead his father's wrath.

As a result, the young Butler emigrated in September 1859, on the ship Roman Emperor to New Zealand. In common with many British settlers of privileged origins, he wanted to put as much distance as possible between himself and his family. He was determined to change his life and removing himself from the toxic relationship of family seemed the one thing in his control.

He wrote of his arrival and life as a sheep farmer on Mesopotamia Station in 'A First Year in Canterbury Settlement' (1863). After a few years of farming he sold his farm and made a handsome profit. The chief achievement of these years however was not farming or money but his ability to write. In these years were gathered the source materials and the first drafts for much of his masterpiece 'Erewhon'.

'Erewhon' revealed Butler's long interest in Darwin's theories of biological evolution. In 1863, four years after Darwin published 'On the Origin of Species', the editor of The Press, a New Zealand newspaper, published a letter titled 'Darwin among the Machines.' Written by Butler but signed Cellarius (q.v.,) it compares human evolution to machine evolution. Rather startlingly it projected that machines would eventually replace man: "In the course of ages we shall find ourselves the inferior race."

But Butler was not a devoted admirer of Darwin. Indeed he spent much time criticising him. In part this was due to Butler's complicated relationship with his own father and grandfather percolating through. He was of the belief that Darwin had used some of the work pioneered by his own father and grandfather and not sufficiently credited it. Butler was an evolutionist, just not of the Darwin kind.

Butler returned to England in 1864, settling in rooms in Clifford's Inn, near Fleet Street, where he would live for the rest of his life.

In 1872, he published his Utopian novel 'Erewhon' anonymously, causing some speculation as to the identity of the author. When Butler revealed himself, 'Erewhon' made him a well-known figure, more because of this speculation than for its literary merits, which remain undisputed.

In 1839 his grandfather Dr Butler had left Samuel property he owned at Whitehall in Shrewsbury on the condition that he survived his own father and his aunt, Dr Butler's daughter Harriet Lloyd. While at Cambridge in 1857 he sold the Whitehall mansion and six acres to his cousin Thomas Bucknall Lloyd, but kept the remaining land surrounding the mansion. His aunt died in 1880 and his father's death in 1886 resolved his financial problems for the last sixteen years of his own life.

There has been some speculation as to why Butler never married. For many years he made regular visits to a woman, Lucie Dumas, where he paid for sex but this seems overshadowed by his intense male friendships, which is reflected in several of his works.

His first significant male friendship was with the young Charles Pauli, whom he met in New Zealand; they both returned to England in 1864 and took neighbouring apartments in Clifford's Inn. Butler now paid Pauli a regular pension to finance his study of the law. This payment continued long after the friendship had cooled. With Pauli's death in 1892, Butler was shocked to learn that Pauli had benefited from mirror arrangements with other men and had died wealthy. He left nothing to Butler.

After 1878, Butler became close friends with Henry Festing Jones. Butler took him on as his literary assistant and travelling companion, at a salary of £200 a year. Jones kept his own lodgings but the two men saw each other daily, working together on music and writing projects during the day, and attending concerts and the theatre in the evenings. They were also frequent visitors to Europe. After Butler's death, Jones edited Butler's notebooks for publication and later published his own biography of Butler in 1919.

Butler was partial to indulging himself, holidaying in Italy every summer and producing his works on the Italian landscape and art. His close interest in the art of the Sacri Monti is reflected in 'Alps and Sanctuaries of Piedmont' and the 'Canton Ticino' (1881) and 'Ex Voto' (1888).

Another significant friendship was with Hans Rudolf Faesch, a Swiss student who stayed with them in London for two years, improving his English, before departing East for Singapore. Butler and Jones both wept when he left on his travels in early 1895. Butler subsequently wrote a very emotional poem, "In

Memoriam H. R. F.", which was offered for publication to several leading English magazines. With the Oscar Wilde trial, and its revelations of homosexual behaviour among the literati now being aired, Butler feared association and hastily withdrew the poem.

He wrote a number of other books, including a moderately successful sequel, 'Erewhon Revisited'. His masterpiece and semi-autobiographical novel 'The Way of All Flesh' did not appear in print until after his death. Butler thought its tone of satirical attack on Victorian morality too contentious and shied away from further potential problems.

Samuel Butler died aged 66 on 18th June 1902 at a nursing home in St John's Wood Road, London. He was cremated at Woking Crematorium, and accounts say his ashes were either dispersed or buried in an unmarked grave.

George Bernard Shaw and E.M. Forster were great admirers of the later works of Samuel Butler, who brought a new form into Victorian literature of utopian/dystopian literature.

Butler belonged to no literary school, and although respected was not the subject of any literary devotion during his lifetime. Although an amateur student of religion and evolution his writings and controversial assertions shut him out from these opposing factions of church and science which played such a large role in late Victorian cultural life: "In those days one was either a religionist or a Darwinian, but he was neither." His later influence on literature came mainly through 'The Way of All Flesh', which Butler began in 1870 and finished after some revisions in 1885 but was unpublished on his explicit wishes until 1903. Despite the decades of its incubation it was still fresh and modern especially in its use of psychoanalytical thought.

Whether it be in his satire and fiction, his studies on the evidences of Christianity, his works on evolutionary thought or in his various other writings, a consistent theme runs through Butler's work, stemming largely from his personal struggle with the stifling of his own nature by his parents, which led him on to seek more general principles of growth, development and purpose. That struggle resulted in a literary career that is still respected to this day.

Samuel Butler – A Concise Bibliography

Darwin among the Machines (1863, largely incorporated into Erewhon)
Lucubratio Ebria (1865)
Erewhon, or Over the Range (1872)
Life and Habit (1878).
Evolution, Old and New; Or, the theories of Buffon, Dr. Erasmus Darwin, and Lamarck, as compared with that of Charles Darwin (1879)
Unconscious Memory (1880)
Alps and Sanctuaries of Piedmont and the Canton Ticino (1881)
Luck or Cunning as the Main Means of Organic Modification? (1887)
Ex Voto; An Account of the Sacro Monte or New Jerusalem at Verallo-Sesia (1888)
The Authoress of the Odyssey (1897)
The Iliad of Homer, Rendered into English Prose (1898)
Shakespeare's Sonnets Reconsidered (1899)

The Odyssey of Homer (1900)

Erewhon Revisited Twenty Years Later: By the Original Discoverer of the Country & His Son (1901)

The Way of All Flesh (1903, also entitled Ernest Pontifex; or, The Way of All Flesh)

God the Known and God the Unknown (1909)

The Note-Books of Samuel Butler (1912)

The Fair Haven (1913, considers inconsistencies between the Gospels)

A First Year in Canterbury Settlement With Other Early Essays (1914)

www.ingramcontent.com/pod-product-compliance
Lightning Source LLC
Chambersburg PA
CBHW060108050426

42448CB00011B/2654